THE 12 BIGGEST BREAKTHROUGHS IN
MILITARY TECHNOLOGY

by Vicki C. Hayes

12 STORY LIBRARY

www.12StoryLibrary.com

Copyright © 2019 by 12-Story Library, Mankato, MN 56003. All rights reserved. No part of this book may be reproduced or utilized in any form or by any means without written permission from the publisher.

12-Story Library is an imprint of Bookstaves.

Photographs ©: MR1805/iStockphoto, cover, 1; Masson/Shutterstock.com, 4; Sergei Prokhorov/Shutterstock.com, 4; Charles Hoffman/CC2.0, 5; ArtMari/Shutterstock.com, 6; Gordan/Shutterstock.com, 7; Max Smith/PD, 8; The London Stereoscopic and Photographic Co./PD, 9; Andrew Skudder/CC2.0, 10; US Army, 11; PD, 12; Master Sgt. Andy Dunaway/ US Air Force, 13; Everett Historical/Shutterstock.com, 13; Ensign Dusan Ilic/US Navy, 14; Mass Communication Specialist Second Class Aidan P. Campbell/US Navy, 15; PD, 16; National Museum of the US Navy, 17; PD, 18; MR. Yanukit/Shutterstock.com, 19; offlinesk/ Shutterstock.com, 19; Everett Historical/Shutterstock.com, 20; Zack Frank/Shutterstock. com, 21; Vincent Grebenicek/Shutterstock.com, 21; British Army/PD, 22; Tech. Sgt. Matt Hecht/US National Guard, 23; Fotosr52/Shutterstock.com, 23; Northrop Grumman/ National Museum of the US Air Force, 24; Africa Studio/Shutterstock.com, 25; Gorodenkoff/ Shutterstock.com, 26; sdecoret/Shutterstock.com, 27; DutchScenery/Shutterstock.com, 28; NASA, 29

ISBN
978-1-63235-583-6 (hardcover)
978-1-63235-637-6 (paperback)
978-1-63235-697-0 (ebook)

Library of Congress Control Number: 2018945325

Printed in the United States of America
Mankato, MN
June 2018

Access free, up-to-date content on this topic plus a full digital version of this book. Scan the QR code on page 31 or use your school's login at 12StoryLibrary.com.

Table of Contents

Plate Armor Protects the Body from Injury

Warfare is when nations have armed conflicts. All through history, people have had wars. At first, they used whatever weapons were around. They used sticks and rocks. But over the years, military technology has changed a lot.

One of the first inventions to change the way wars were fought was armor. Armor was made to protect the body from injury. There were two types of armor. Chain mail was made up of many small rings of metal. The rings were wired together. Knights in the Middle Ages wore chain mail suits. Well-made chain mail could stop swords and spears.

Plate armor was made of plates of metal. The plates were pounded and shaped by hand. At first, the plates were sewn into clothes. Later they were joined together with leather or brass buckles. Plate armor could cover the whole body. There were special pieces to cover sensitive body parts. These were places like armpits, elbows, and knees.

Chain mail and plate armor were popular from the twelfth to fourteenth centuries. Armor worked very well to protect

This horse and body armor from 1507 weighs almost 100 pounds (50 kg).

45-55
Weight in pounds (20–25 kg) of an average suit of armor in the 1400s.

- Chain mail was made of tiny rings of metal.
- Chain mail could block swords and spears.
- Plate armor offered better protection but was very heavy.
- Weapons were invented that could pierce armor.

knights from punctures and crushing. It stopped bullets from early firearms. It stopped arrows from crossbows. Armor protected horses from lances. But armor had one problem. It was very heavy. Then it had another problem. Weapons were developed that could pierce armor. These included the longbow and powerful rifles. By the end of the eighteenth century, armor was used more for decoration than protection.

5

2

Gunpowder Explodes on the Scene

Gunpowder was invented by the Chinese in the ninth century. Alchemists were looking for a way to help people live longer. They mixed together saltpeter, sulfur, and charcoal. The result was a powder that exploded.

For the next 400 years, the Chinese used gunpowder to fight their wars. They would put tubes of gunpowder on arrows. The gunpowder would ignite as it flew toward the enemy. This invention was called flying fire.

In the thirteenth century, gunpowder spread to Europe. In the fifteenth century, gunpowder was used in guns. The gunpowder would ignite in the gun barrel. The explosion would propel bullets faster and further. These bullets could pass through armor. Gunpowder was also used in cannons. Cannonballs could knock down castle walls. Fortifications and armor were no longer good protections.

Early gunpowder was a black powder. It was called a low explosive. It worked well, but it could be dangerous. Black powder is still used for signal flares, blanks, and fireworks. But today almost all ammunition is smokeless powder. There are over 100 kinds. They have different burning rates. Different powders work better in different types of guns.

Warships could fire a broadside. All guns along one side of the ship would fire at once.

MEN-OF-WAR

In the sixteenth century, the English built large warships called men-of-war. A man-of-war had many cannons and guns mounted on its deck. Gunpowder was used to hurl iron balls at other ships. These balls weighed 30 to 50 pounds (13–22 kg). The best warship of England's King Henry VIII had 186 guns. By 1900, England had used these ships to win sea battles all over the world.

100
Number of smokeless gunpowders used in weapons today.

- Gunpowder was invented by the Chinese.
- Gunpowder made guns and cannons very powerful.
- Early gunpowder was a black powder.
- Weapons today use smokeless powder.

3

Machine Guns Increase the Speed of Battle

A machine gun is a gun that fires automatically. A machine gun can fire 500 to 1000 bullets in a minute. It fires as long as the trigger is held down. It stops when the bullets are gone. Machine guns were invented in the late nineteenth century. There are different types of machine guns. Some can be run by one person. Some need a team of people.

Early machine guns had revolving cylinders. The cylinder fed bullets into the gun's chamber. The Gatling gun was an early type of machine gun. It was used in the American Civil War. But these guns were clumsy and unreliable. Smokeless powder helped to make a better machine gun. Smokeless powder burned evenly. This kept the moving parts moving together. Hiram Maxim invented the first fully automatic

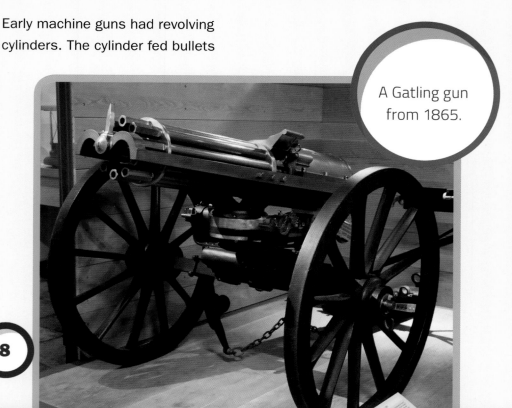

A Gatling gun from 1865.

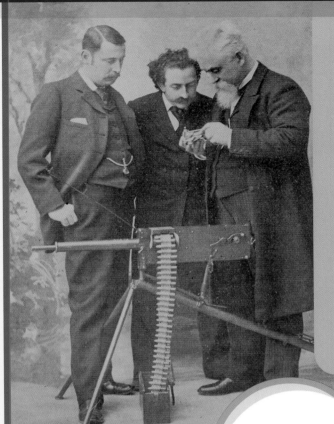

1884

Year the first machine gun was invented by Hiram Maxim.

- Machine guns fire automatically.
- They were very common in World War I.
- At first, machine guns needed several operators.
- WWI airplanes had mounted machine guns.

Hiram Maxim demonstrates his machine gun.

machine gun. It used smokeless powder.

Machine guns were very common in World War I. This war was sometimes called the "machine gun war." World War I machine guns were mounted on tripods. The guns needed four to six operators. Eventually smaller guns were invented. They could be used by one person.

World War I fighter pilots wanted machine guns. They wanted to shoot down other planes. But WWI planes had front propellers. How could a machine gun fire between the propeller blades? Soon a way was invented. It synchronized the firing with the propellers.

Tanks Roll onto the Battlefield

A tank is a vehicle used in combat. It can withstand enemy fire. Tanks are covered with armor. They have lots of weapons. Tanks don't have wheels. They move on a continuously rolling track. This helps tanks travel over all sorts of land. They can also crush barbed wire.

The first tank was made by the British Army in 1915. It was called Little Willie. It was not a success. It moved very slowly. It got stuck a lot. But improvements were made.

Early tanks traveled 2 miles (3 km) an hour. But soon they could go 20 miles (32 km) an hour. Tanks became stronger. They carried more weapons. They became very important in battles. In World War II, Germany had powerful tanks called panzers. Other countries also used tanks. Many tanks had rotating turrets.

Tank technology has continued to improve. Today's tanks have thermal imaging and digital firing. They have

CHARIOTS

The first vehicles used on the battlefield were chariots. Chariots were used over 4,000 years ago. They were in places like Egypt, Greece, China, and India. Chariots were pulled by horses. They usually carried two people. One was the driver. The other held a bow and arrow or javelin. Chariots gave armies the ability to move quickly. People stopped using chariots when they started riding horses.

6,506
Number of tanks made by France and Great Britain by the end of WWI.

- Tanks stand up under enemy fire.
- They move on tracks instead of wheels.
- Tanks carry large guns and have rotating turrets.
- Tank technology continues to improve.

laser rangefinders. They can hide from radar. Future improvements include rocket grenades and stealth technologies.

The M1A2 SEP battle tank is the backbone of the US armored forces today.

Airplanes Move Warfare into the Skies

The Wright brothers made the first airplane flight in 1903. Over the next 10 years, airplane technology boomed. In World War I, airplanes were an important part of the military. They were used to observe the enemy. They were used to drop bombs. They were used for rescue. They had guns to shoot down other planes.

By the beginning of World War II, fighter planes were better.

300,000
Number of military aircraft produced by the United States during World War II.

- Early fighter planes were used for observation and rescue.
- Some planes dropped bombs.
- Battles between planes were called dogfights.
- Today's fighter jets are very fast and powerful.

The 1915 Fokker Eindecker plane had a synchronized machine gun.

The F16-Fighting Falcon is one of the most advanced combat aircrafts today.

AIRSHIPS

Before WWI, the military used airships. An airship had a rigid frame covered with fabric. Inside the frame was hydrogen. Hydrogen is a gas that is lighter than air. These large aircraft would fly over enemy locations. They would drop bombs. The biggest of these airships were made by Count Ferdinand von Zeppelin. Airships were powerful, but they were also dangerous. The hydrogen inside could explode. Airships stopped being used after fighter planes were developed.

They were faster, stronger, and had more guns. They had names like Spitfire, Mustang, Zero, and Hurricane. Sometimes these planes would battle each other at close range. This was called a dogfight.

The first planes flew at 70 miles (112 km) an hour. Today's jets fly at over 1,000 miles (1,600 km) an hour. They can turn, dive, and flip at these speeds. They use modern electronics to find enemy targets. They have powerful weapons to destroy their targets. Much of what they do is very complex. Humans can no longer keep up. There is still a pilot on board. But many of the systems on a fighter jet are automated.

6

Aircraft Carriers Transport Jets Around the World

Aircraft carriers are very large ships. They carry planes. The planes take off from and land on the ships. The top deck of an aircraft carrier is called the flight deck. The hangar deck is lower. It is where planes are usually stored.

Planes need a long runway to take off. Even the biggest aircraft carrier does not have a long enough deck. To help planes take off, carriers use catapults. A catapult has a tow bar. The tow bar is connected to the plane. The pilot gets the plane's engines up to a high rate of speed. Then the catapult flings the plane forward. Everything has to be done exactly right. If not, the plane may be flung into the ocean.

Landing on an aircraft carrier is also tricky. The runway is only about 500 feet (150 meters) long. To land on

A tailhook on the jet must catch one of four cables when landing on a carrier.

a flight deck, a jet uses a tailhook. A tailhook is a hook hanging down from the plane's tail. Stretched across the flight deck are four very strong cables. The pilot has a hard job. He has to get the tailhook to catch one of the four cables. The cables help to slow the plane down.

The largest aircraft carrier today is the USS *Gerald R. Ford.* It can carry 75 aircraft and over 4,500 people.

THINK ABOUT IT

Working on an aircraft carrier is very exciting. It is also very dangerous. Why do you think someone would put up with danger in order to have excitement?

20
Number of aircraft carriers in the world in 2018.

- Aircraft carriers are like large floating islands.
- They carry planes around the world.
- Planes need catapults to take off from a carrier.
- They need tailhooks to land.

Submarines Go to Great Depths to Aid the Military

Submarines are large, powerful ships. They can travel underwater. Subs have many uses. One use is to protect aircraft carriers. Submarines can travel in secret. They can attack ships that threaten the aircraft carriers. Subs have other uses, too. They spy on the enemy. They lay underwater mines. They deliver people and supplies without being detected.

The first submarine was invented in the 1620s. A Dutch man named Cornelius van Drebel had a covered boat. He rowed his boat 12 to 15 feet (4 to 5 m) underwater. The first war submarine was used during the American Revolution. It was called the Turtle. Its job was to attach gunpowder to an enemy ship. It was not successful.

Modern subs can stay underwater because they have ballasts. Ballasts are big tanks that fill up with water. As the ballasts on a sub fill, the sub sinks. Then the water gets pumped out of the ballasts. This lets the sub rise to the surface.

Deep in the ocean, it is dark. Subs use sonar to find their way.

In 1775, the Turtle failed at fastening mines to ships.

Sonar bounces sound waves off objects. Subs also use sonar to find enemy ships. Early submarines were powered by batteries and diesel fuel. Today's subs use nuclear power. Big military submarines can have a crew of 100 people. These subs can stay underwater for months at a time.

THINK ABOUT IT

Life on a submarine is cramped. Sailors might not get off the sub for days or even weeks. How do you think they cope with this?

2011

Year women were first allowed to serve on US Navy submarines.

- Submarines are ships that travel underwater.
- The military use subs for spying and attacking.
- Big tanks, or ballasts, allow subs to rise and sink.
- Subs use sonar to "see" underwater.

US Navy Seawolf nuclear-powered submarines are the most advanced in the world.

Radar Detects Hidden Enemies

Radar can detect objects that can't be seen. Using radar is like using a flashlight. But radar uses radio waves instead of light. Radar stands for Radio Detection and Ranging. Radar can identify an object. Radar knows its location and its speed. It can "see" through darkness and fog. It can see over long distances.

Many scientists had been studying radio waves. They knew some objects reflected radio waves. Robert Watson-Watt was a Scottish inventor. He wanted to invent a "death ray" using radio waves. Instead, he discovered radar. In 1935, he got a patent for his invention. The British used radar in World War II. They used it to protect their coast. Radar detected planes up to 200 miles (320 km)

Soldiers at a radar during World War II, watching for approaching airplanes.

away. This gave the British lots of warning. They sent their planes out early. Their planes were able to meet and shoot down German planes.

Radar technology has improved over the years. Today the military uses radar on many of its guided missiles. It also uses radar in its Ballistic Missile Early Warning System.

STEALTH TECHNOLOGY

When a new technology is invented, an opposite technology is often invented. The military used radar a lot. But they also wanted a way to hide from radar. Stealth technology was invented. Stealth aircraft are shaped differently. Radar waves reflect off at an angle. Stealth aircraft are made of new materials. These materials absorb radar waves. Stealth technology makes aircraft invisible to radar.

Air Defense Radar

WARNING
Ballistic Missile

-Type: Intercontinental ballistic missile.
-Range: 8,100 miles (13,000 km).
-Weight: 78,000 lb (35,300 kg).
-Length: 59 ft 9.5 in (18.2 m).
-Diameter: 5 ft 6 in (1.7 m) (1st stage).
-Warhead: Nuclear.
-Speed: Mach 23, or 28,176 km/h, or 7.8 km/s

Nuclear Weapons Threaten the World

All matter in the universe is made up of atoms. Atoms can be split or combined. Splitting atoms is called fission. Combining atoms is called fusion. Both fission and fusion release huge amounts of energy. This energy has been used to create bombs. These bombs are nuclear weapons.

15,000
Approximate number of nuclear weapons in the world today.

- Nuclear bombs use either fission or fusion.
- Only two nuclear bombs have ever been used.
- Eight countries have nuclear weapons.
- Nuclear weapons are incredibly powerful.

Mushroom cloud from the bombing of Nagasaki, Japan, on August 9, 1945.

The first nuclear bomb exploded in 1945. It was in New Mexico. It was a test by the United States Army. One month later, two more nuclear bombs exploded. They were dropped on Japan by the United States. This led to the end of World War II. Since then, nuclear weapons have been tested. But they have not been used in war. Eight countries have developed nuclear weapons. They are the United States, Russia, France, and Great Britain. The others are China, India, Pakistan, and North Korea.

Nuclear weapons are extremely powerful. The bombs dropped on Japan destroyed whole cities. Between 100,000 and 200,000 people died. More powerful nuclear weapons have been tested. One was 3,333 times bigger than just one of the bombs dropped on Japan.

ARMS RACE

After World War II, the United States and the Soviet Union had the Cold War. This was a race to build weapons. Both countries made thousands of nuclear weapons. Neither country used them. They worried about nuclear war. It was possible no one on Earth would survive. Today many countries have treaties. They promise not to use these weapons. Some nuclear weapons have been taken apart. Not all countries have agreed to these treaties.

Night Vision Finds Objects in the Dark

There are several ways to find objects in the dark. Sonar uses sound waves. Radar uses radio waves. But there is another way. Night vision uses light and heat waves.

Light waves come in different lengths. We can see some light waves. We call these visible light waves. They include the colors red, orange, yellow, green, blue, and violet. But there are light waves longer and shorter than the visible spectrum. Longer waves are called infrared. Infrared waves include heat waves. Many objects, including people, emit heat. Heat waves are also called thermal waves. We can't see heat waves with our eyes. But there are devices that can "see" heat waves. These are called thermal imagers.

Another kind of night vision is amplified light. On a dark night, there may still be a little light. Perhaps there are stars. Night vision goggles or scopes amplify that light. They can make objects look much brighter. They make objects

The Zielgerät 1229 was the first night-vision sniperscope. It was first used in combat in 1945.

1000

Number of feet (300 m) modern night vision headsets can "see" ahead into the dark.

- Many objects emit heat.
- Heat, or infrared waves, can be detected by night vision goggles.
- Other night vision devices amplify available light.
- Today's soldiers use advanced night vision technologies.

20,000 to 50,000 times brighter than the human eye can see.

Night vision was first used by the Germans in the mid-1930s. Soon the technology took off. Soldiers today use thermal imaging and light amplification. Both technologies are together in headsets. The headsets weigh less than a pound. The headsets can run on batteries for eight hours. This technology allows soldiers to find hidden targets.

It helps to keep them from being attacked by surprise. There are also night vision cameras. They can take pictures in the dark.

Satellites Relay Information Around the Globe

23,000
Approximate miles (37,000 km) above the earth where DSCS satellites orbit.

- Satellites help the military with worldwide communication.
- Eight satellites can reach just about anywhere on Earth.
- Satellites are also used for spying and navigation.

Defense satellites detect missile launches, space launches, and nuclear detonations.

Countries sometimes have military forces outside their borders. For example, the United States has military people in over 170 countries. Communication is very important. It must be fast and secure. One of the best ways to communicate is by using satellites.

In 1968, the United States began using a new system. It is called the

Defense Satellite Communication System (DSCS). This system sends data using eight satellites. These satellites can reach everywhere on Earth.

Over the years, engineers have made the satellites more powerful. The satellites can handle more data. They are more secure. The information travels much faster. Information can be sent everywhere. It can travel between ships, airplanes, and the ground. The signals are protected from interception and jamming. The devices that send and receive these communications are small and portable.

The military uses satellites in other ways, too. Some satellites are used for spying. They take pictures of military targets. Some spy satellites look for missiles. They use infrared technology. Some satellites are used for navigation. Submarines often use navigation satellites. This is because these submarines have to stay below water most of the time.

GPS

GPS stands for Global Positioning System. GPS allows anyone to find their position on Earth. It uses 24 satellites. The United States Air Force started using GPS in 1980. Many people have GPS in their cars and phones. These GPS receivers are accurate to 16 feet (5 meters). Military receivers are accurate to a few centimeters (one inch).

Cyber Warfare Attacks from Within

One of the newest types of attacks is cyber warfare. Cyber warfare is when technology is used to attack technology. A computer hacker might break into a bank's computer. Then the hacker could steal money. A hacker might get into a big company's computer. Then the hacker could steal information. A hacker might

26

61,000
Number of cyber attacks on the United States federal government in 2014.

- Cyber warfare is when computers are used to attack other computers.
- Ransomware is when hackers demand money.
- Battling cyber warfare is an ongoing task.

get into a government's computers. Then the hacker could turn off a country's electric power.

Attacks like these have already happened. Many companies and governments are getting attacked. They are working hard to build security programs. These programs will lower the risk of cyber warfare.

Ransomware is another type of cyber warfare. Hackers take control of someone's computer. Then they ask for money. The computer might belong to a person. It might belong to a city. In 2018, hackers took control of a city's computers. They took over the government computers in Atlanta, Georgia. The hackers

demanded $50,000. Then they said they would return control to the city.

Some cyber attackers are individuals. Some are governments of other countries. Computer experts are working hard to stop cyber warfare. They are working on computer defenses. Engineers are looking for weaknesses. Computers are watched more carefully. When there are attacks, the response is quick.

THINK ABOUT IT

People like to shop and talk online. This means they share personal information. Cyber attackers steal personal information. Why do you think people continue to use these services?

Fact Sheet

- Walls were built to keep enemies out. Two famous walls in history were Hadrian's Wall and the Great Wall of China. More modern military uses of fortification include pits and moats, forts and palisade walls, barbed wire and field mines, bunkers and blast doors.

- Many soldiers on the battlefield died because they didn't receive quick treatment. As many as half died from blood loss. Today's battlefield medics get to injured soldiers as quickly as possible. When soldiers receive immediate treatment, they have a better chance of surviving.

- The internal combustion engine works by burning gas or oil. We know the term because private cars have used these engines for years. But a huge amount of military equipment also relies on this engine. This equipment includes tanks, trucks, airplanes, subs, helicopters, and jets.

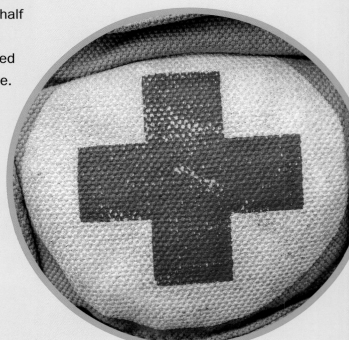

- Photography was invented in 1839. It quickly became an essential military tool. Photographs were used to document military events. Cameras took pictures of enemy troops and military installations. Photographs were used for rescues. Today cameras are in planes and satellites.

- The telegraph (1830s) and radio (1890s) were inventions that expanded communication technology. These were vital to the military. For example, the telegraph was used in the American Civil War to keep track of troop movements. Radio was used in World War I to warn of gas attacks on the front lines.

- Chemicals have been invented to serve many purposes. These include cooking, cleaning, helping plants grow, producing new products, and many more. The military also uses chemicals. Some are developed and used as poisons for warfare. But others are for food preservation, medical care, and for keeping equipment working.

Glossary

alchemist
A person who tries to change one kind of metal into another, or to cure a disease or prolong life with magical means.

amplified
Louder or more intense.

automated
Operated by machines or computers.

ballistic
Having to do with the flight of projectiles through space, like bullets, bombs, or rockets.

catapult
A device used to hurl objects by building up tension and then suddenly releasing it, like a slingshot.

cyber
Having to do with computers or information technology.

jamming
Making radio or radar not work by introducing interference.

mine
Explosive underwater device designed to blow up ships.

palisade
A fence of wooden stakes.

stealth
Using technology that makes it hard to be seen by radar.

synchronize
To make two things work together at the same rate or time.

thermal
Relating to heat.

turret
The movable part on a tank or warship where the guns are fixed.

For More Information

Books

Hale, Nathan. *Treaties, Trenches, Mud, and Blood: A World War I Tale.* New York: Amulet Books, 2014.

Hopkinson, Deborah. *Dive! World War II Stories of Sailors & Submarines in the Pacific.* New York: Scholastic Press, 2016.

Oxlade, Chris. *Inside Fighter Planes.* Lerner Publishing Group: Minneapolis, 2017.

Sheinkin, Steve. *Bomb: The Race to Build – and Steal – the World's Most Dangerous Weapon.* New York: Macmillan, 2012.

Visit 12StoryLibrary.com

Scan the code or use your school's login at **12StoryLibrary.com** for recent updates about this topic and a full digital version of this book. Enjoy free access to:

- Digital ebook
- Breaking news updates
- Live content feeds
- Videos, interactive maps, and graphics
- Additional web resources

Note to educators: Visit 12StoryLibrary.com/register to sign up for free premium website access. Enjoy live content plus a full digital version of every 12-Story Library book you own for every student at your school.

Index

About the Author

Vicki C. Hayes has worked in television and radio in New York and Washington. She has a master's degree in Film and Electronic Media and currently works as a teacher and writer.

READ MORE FROM 12-STORY LIBRARY

Every 12-Story Library Book is available in many fomats. For more information, visit 12StoryLibrary.com